Midsummer Night's Dream

A Shakespeare Story

RETOLD BY ANDREW MATTHEWS
ILLUSTRATED BY TONY ROSS

ORCHARD

To Hannah, love you more than...
A.M.

For Laura K.
T.R.

ORCHARD BOOKS
338 Euston Road, London NW1 3BH
Orchard Books Australia
Hachette Children's Books
Level 17/207 Kent St, Sydney, NSW 2000
This text was first published in Great Britain in the form of a gift collection
called The Orchard Book of Shakespeare Stories, illustrated by
Angela Barrett in 2001.
This edition first published in hardback in Great Britain in 2002
First paperback publication in 2003
This slipcase edition published in 2013
Not for individual resale
Text © Andrew Matthews 2001
Illustrations © Tony Ross 2002
ISBN 978 1 40780 989 2
The rights of Andrew Matthews to be identified as the author and Tony Ross as
the illustrator of this work have been asserted by them in accordance with the
Copyright, Designs and Patents Act, 1988
A CIP catalogue record for this book is available from the British Library
Printed in China

Orchard Books is a division of Hachette Childrens Books,
an Hachette UK company.
www.hachette.co.uk

Contents

Cast List

Hermia
In love with Lysander

Helena
Friend to Hermia
In love with Demetrius

Demetrius
Betrothed to Hermia

Lysander
In love with Hermia

Oberon

King of the Fairies

Titania

Queen of the Fairies

Puck

An Elf

Bottom

A Weaver

The Scene

In and around Athens, Ancient Greece.

Ay me, for aught that I could ever read,
Could ever hear by tale or history,
The course of true love never did run smooth,

Lysander; I.i.

A Midsummer Night's Dream

When the path of true love runs smoothly, the world seems a wonderful place – all bright skies and smiling faces.

Unfortunately, true love has a habit of wandering off the path and getting lost, and when that happens people's lives get lost too, in a tangle of misery.

Take the love
of Duke Theseus
of Athens and
Hippolyta, Queen
of the Amazons, for
instance. They were to
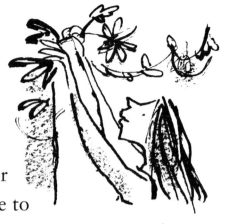
be married, and their happiness spread
through the whole of Athens. People had
decorated their houses with flowers, and
left lamps burning in their windows at
night, so that the streets twinkled like a
city of stars. Everybody
was joyful and excited
as they prepared to
celebrate the Duke's
wedding day.
Well, almost
everybody…

8

On the day before the royal wedding, two friends met by chance in the market square: golden-haired Hermia, and black-haired Helena, both beautiful and both with secrets that made their hearts ache.

For a while, the two friends chatted about nothing in particular. Then Helena noticed a look in Hermia's deep blue eyes that made her ask, "Is everything all right, Hermia?"

Hermia looked so sad and serious.

"I am to marry Demetrius tomorrow," she replied.

"Demetrius!" said Helena softly. Now her heart was aching worse than ever. Night after night she had cried herself to sleep, whispering Demetrius's name, knowing that her love for him was hopeless.

Many years ago the families of Hermia and Demetrius had agreed that, when they were of age, their daughter and son should marry. "You must be the happiest young woman in Athens!" sighed Helena.

"I've never been so miserable in my life!" Hermia declared. "You see, I don't love Demetrius."

"You don't?" cried Helena, amazed.

"I'm in love with Lysander," Hermia confessed, and she began to describe all the things that made Lysander so wonderful.

Helena thought about Lysander, with his curly brown hair and broad smile. He was *quite* handsome, she supposed, but he didn't have Demetrius's dark, brooding good looks. Why on earth did Hermia find him so attractive?

"Of course, I told my father that I didn't wish to marry Demetrius," Hermia said, "and he went straight to him to

explain – but you know how stubborn
Demetrius can be. He lost his temper and
said it didn't matter who I loved, our
marriage had been arranged and it must
go ahead, no matter what. His stupid
pride's been hurt, that's all – he doesn't
love me a bit."

"Then who does he love?" Helena
enquired eagerly.

"No one, except for
himself," said Hermia.
"I *can't* marry
someone I don't
love, and I know it
will cause a scandal,
but Lysander and I
are going to run
away together!"

"*When*?" Helena asked.

"Tonight," Hermia told her. "I'm meeting him at midnight in the wood outside the city walls. We plan to travel through the night, and in the morning we'll find a little temple where we can be married. Oh, Helena, it will be so *romantic*! Please say that you're happy for me!"

"Of course I am," said Helena. "I'm overjoyed."

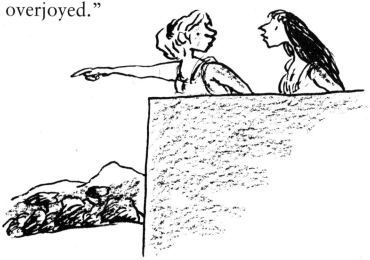

And she was overjoyed – for herself. 'At last, this is my chance!' she thought.

'If I visit Demetrius tonight and tell him that Hermia and Lysander have gone off together, he'll forget about his pride...and then...when I tell him how I feel about him, he'll be so flattered, he'll fall in love with me. Love always finds a way!'

Which is true, but love doesn't always find the way that people expect, as Helena was about to find out. For it was not only in the human world that love was causing unhappiness; although Helena and Hermia did not know it, two different worlds would meet in the wood outside Athens that night, and the result would be chaos.

✳ ✳ ✳

Oberon, King of
the Fairies, was
a creature of
darkness and
shadows, while his
wife, Queen Titania,
was moonlight and
silver. The two loved each

other dearly, but they had quarrelled
bitterly. Titania had taken
a little orphan boy as a
page, and made such
a fuss of the lad
that Oberon
had become
very jealous.
He wanted
the page
for himself.

That midsummer's night, in a clearing in the wood, Titania was singing to her page, while fairy servants fluttered around her like glittering moths.

When Oberon appeared, Titania's silvery eyes darkened. "Fairies, let us leave this place at once!" she said haughtily.

"Wait, Titania!" snapped Oberon.
"This quarrel of ours has gone on long
enough. You say I have no reason to be
jealous of the boy – very well, prove it!
Give him to me!"

"Not for all your fairy kingdom!"
hissed Titania. She raised her left hand,
and sent a ball of blue fire roaring across
the glade, straight at Oberon's head.

Oberon spoke a word of magic, and the fire turned to water that burst over him, drenching his clothes. By the time he had rubbed the water from his eyes, the glade was empty and Oberon was alone. "I'll make you sorry for this, Titania!" he vowed. Then, lifting his dripping head, he called out, "Puck? Come to me, now!"

A breeze sighed in the branches, as an elf dropped out of the air and landed at Oberon's feet. The elf was dressed in leaves that had been sewn together. His hair was tangled, his skin as brown as chestnuts, and when he smiled, his white teeth flashed mischievously.

"Command me, master!" Puck said.

"I mean to teach the Queen a lesson," said Oberon. "Go, search the Earth and fetch me the flower called Love in Idleness."

"I will fly faster than a falling star!" said Puck, and with that he had vanished.

A cruel smile played on Oberon's lips. "When Titania is asleep, I will drop the juice of the flower in her eyes," he said to himself. "Its magic will make her fall in love with the first living thing she sees when she wakes – perhaps a toad, or even a spider! She will make herself seem so ridiculous, that she will beg me to break the spell, and I will...after she's given me the page!"

This plan pleased Oberon so much that he began to laugh – but his laugh was cut short when he heard human voices approaching. With a wave of his fingers, Oberon made himself vanish among the shadows.

Demetrius, out searching for Hermia, halted in the middle of the glade, while he considered which path to take. This gave Helena a chance to catch up with him. "Wait for me, Demetrius!" she pleaded.

Demetrius scowled at her. "For the last time, Helena, go home!" he shouted angrily. "I can find Lysander and Hermia without your help."

"But you don't understand!" Helena exclaimed. "I love you! I've always loved you!"

She tried to put her arms around Demetrius, but he ducked away.

"Well I don't love you!" he said roughly. "So go away and leave me alone!"

And he ran off through the moonlight.

"Oh, Demetrius!" sobbed Helena, running after him. "I would follow you through fire, just to be near you!"

* * *

When the glade was once more still and silent, Oberon came out of the darkness. His face was thoughtful. "I must help that lovely maiden!" he whispered. "I know how cruel it is to love someone whose heart is so cold."

A wind brushed the Fairy King's cheek, and there stood Puck, holding a sprig of glimmering white flowers.

"Take two blossoms and search the woods for a young human couple," Oberon said to him. "Squeeze the juice of the petals into the young man's eyes, but do it when you are sure that the maiden will be the first thing he sees."

"At once, master!" Puck said with a bow, and then he was gone.

Then Oberon went to find Titania.
He found her sleeping alone on a bank of
violets, and the air was heavy with their
sweet perfume. As he dropped juice from
the magic flowers on to Titania's eyelids,
Oberon murmured:

"What you see when you awake,
Do it for your true love take!"

At that very moment, in another part of
the wood, Puck was putting magic juice
into the eyes of a young man he had
found sleeping next to a young woman at
the foot of a pine tree.

"When he wakes and sees her, his love
for her will drive him mad!" Puck giggled,
and he leapt into the air, like a grasshopper
in a summer meadow.

But, as bad luck would have it, Puck had found the wrong couple. Those sleeping under the tree were Lysander and Hermia, who had got lost in the wood and exhausted themselves trying to find the way out.

And as bad luck would also have it, a few seconds after Puck had left them, Helena wandered by, searching for Demetrius. Blinded by tears, Helena did not notice Lysander and Hermia until she stumbled over Lysander's legs.

He woke, saw her, and his eyes bulged like a frog's as the magic went to work.

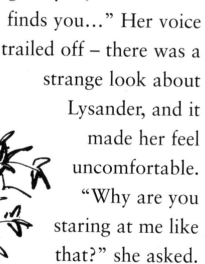

"Lysander?" gasped Helena. "What are you doing here? I mean, you mustn't be here! Get away quickly! Demetrius is looking for you, and if he finds you..." Her voice trailed off – there was a strange look about Lysander, and it made her feel uncomfortable. "Why are you staring at me like that?" she asked.

"Because at last I have found my own true love," said Lysander. "Helena, can't you see how much I love you?"

Helena stepped back, laughing nervously. "Don't be silly, Lysander!" she said. "You love Hermia...don't you?"

"Hermia, who is she?" scoffed Lysander, scrambling to his feet. "How could I love anyone but you, with your eyes like stars, your hair as black as ravens' wings, and your skin as soft as...?"

"That's quite enough of that!" said Helena. "This is some sort of midsummer madness!"

"Madness? Yes, I'm mad!" said Lysander. "Mad with love for you! Come to my arms, and cool the fires of my passion with your kisses!"

He moved towards Helena, but she turned and fled. Lysander followed her, shouting, "There's no escape from love, Helena! This was meant to be!"

Their loud voices and pounding footsteps woke Hermia. "Lysander, where are you?" she muttered sleepily. "Don't wander off on your own, my love. You might be eaten by a lion, or a bear..." The very thought made her wide awake, and she sat up. "Or I might be eaten, come to that!" she said with a shudder. "I'm coming to find you, Lysander, so we can be eaten together!"

✳ ✳ ✳

Not five paces from the bank of
violets where Titania lay asleep, a group
of Athenians had gathered in secret to
rehearse a play that they meant to perform
for Duke Theseus after his wedding. One
of the actors, a weaver called Bottom, was
behind a tree, waiting to appear
when he heard his cue.
"I'll show them how
it's done!" Bottom
said to himself.
"When the Duke
sees what a fine
actor I am, he'll
give me a purse
of gold, or my
name's not
Nick Bottom!"